BE · AN · EXPERT
NATURALIST

JOHN STIDWORTHY

GLOUCESTER PRESS
London · New York · Toronto · Sydney

574

© Aladdin Books Ltd 1991
All rights reserved

Designed and produced by
NW Books Ltd
28 Percy St
London
W1P 9FF

First published in Great
Britain in 1991
by Franklin Watts
96 Leonard Street
London EC2A 4RH

ISBN 0-7496-0601-0

Design David West
Children's Book Design
Designer Stephen
Woosnam-Savage
Editorial Lionheart Books
Picture Researcher
Emma Krikler
Consultant Dr R.W. Forrest
Illustrator Ian Moores
Editor Roger Vlitos

A CIP catalogue record for
this book is available from
the British Library

Printed in Belgium

Photocredits
Pages 5 and 13: Bruce Coleman Limited;
page 10: Eye Ubiquitous; pages 12, 20 and
27: Roger Vlitos; page 23: Robert Harding
Picture Library.

INTRODUCTION

This book is about exploring and understanding the world of nature wherever you may be. With it you can make exciting discoveries that will set you on the road to becoming an expert naturalist. Within the habitats described, we have taken a representative cross-section of animals and plants. Your own area may have a different variety of species. Don't worry, this is all part of the fun of discovering the natural world. We show you how to make "field" notes and drawings of what you have come across so that you can refer to a comprehensive guidebook later on.

There are a variety of projects here which will help you learn about the animals, plants and their habitats. However, an important part of being a naturalist is taking care not to disturb or harm creatures in the wild. For example, we ask you to put back rocks you have turned over in tide pools and return frogs to the ponds where you may have collected them as tadpoles. Remember, always follow the naturalist's code (see page 31).

CONTENTS

FRESHWATER PONDS
4
Fish, Plants & Small Animals
Amphibians and Birds
Making a Pond Environment
5-11
WOODLAND LIFE
12
Wildlife, Plants & Insects
Birds and Mammals
Reptiles & Making an Ants' Nest
13-19
SEASHORE LIFE
20
Plants, Birds & Fish
Shelled Animals
Rockpool Study
21-25
IN TOWNS
26
Gardens
In the House
27-29
KEEPING RECORDS
30
EQUIPMENT
31
GLOSSARY & INDEX
32

FRESHWATER PONDS

Ponds are "home" to a wide variety of creatures from fish and birds to insects and worms. If you look more carefully in the water, or even amongst the mud at the bottom, you can discover tiny creatures which in spite of their size are very important to the pond's life.

A pond is at its busiest in spring and summer, when animals such as toads and dragonflies are breeding, and plants are growing quickly. In the winter many of the pond's inhabitants lie dormant. Animals such as frogs hibernate in the mud. Water plants may be "resting" too. But when spring comes, a vigorous new life returns to the pond.

A POND SURVEY

Small ponds can be "mapped" to show their shape, depth, and also which plants grow where. Measure the width and use squared paper to draw a detailed outline. Use a ruler to measure the depth and note where the plants grow. Some kinds prefer deep water, others have floating leaves or flowers.

Check the pond's edges for footprints left by birds, water voles and other animals.

Polaroid sunglasses, or a plastic box held in the water, help you to see past the surface reflections.

Ruler

Thermometers

WARNING: PONDS CAN BE DANGEROUS.

Bulrush

Belted kingfisher

Damsel fly

Common frog

Common newt

Great diving beetle

Horse leech

Salamander

FOOD WEBS

All the plants and animals that you can see below are part of the pond's complex "food web".

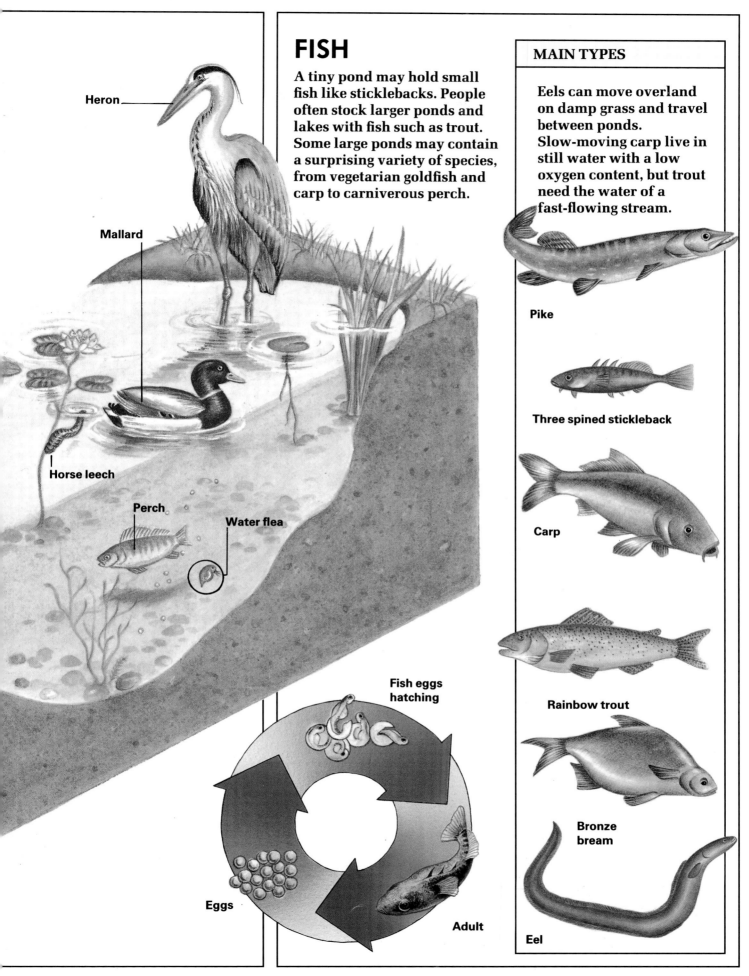

FISH

A tiny pond may hold small fish like sticklebacks. People often stock larger ponds and lakes with fish such as trout. Some large ponds may contain a surprising variety of species, from vegetarian goldfish and carp to carniverous perch.

Heron

Mallard

Horse leech

Perch

Water flea

Fish eggs hatching

Eggs

Adult

MAIN TYPES

Eels can move overland on damp grass and travel between ponds. Slow-moving carp live in still water with a low oxygen content, but trout need the water of a fast-flowing stream.

Pike

Three spined stickleback

Carp

Rainbow trout

Bronze bream

Eel

PLANTS

Large numbers of flowering plants grow in and around ponds and lakes. Plants growing in water do not need a strong stem for support. Some even have air-spaces in their stems to help them float towards the light. Many water plants have feathery or ribbon-like leaves. These are usually found in flowing water but can survive in small ponds. Some water plants grow right up to the surface, and push their flowers into the air. These often have different shaped leaves above and below water. Roots are not necessary to get water into an underwater plant's body, but most varieties of water plant still have roots to anchor them to the bottom. Some kinds, though, float at the water's surface.

Try to study and draw a pond's plants. Check if they are anchored underwater or floating on the surface.

TYPES AND ZONES

Plant zones can be seen in a pond. Plants such as kingcups like the marshy edges. Reeds and bulrushes need their roots in water. Others, such as Canadian pond weed, grow totally submerged.

Bulrush

White water lily

Water soldier

Frogbit

Canadian pond weed

In a well-planted garden pond the plants will be zoned as they are in a natural pond.

Arrowhead

Bulrush

Frogbit

Club rush

Water lily

Hornwort

Canadian pond weed

SMALL ANIMALS

Apart from the wide variety of microscopic creatures, many kinds of small animals can be found in most ponds. Snails, for example, eat algae and the slimy film which covers the surface of plants growing in water. They have file-like tongues which scrape these foods off rocks or leaves.

Segmented worms are also common in ponds. Some look very much like earthworms. Other types are thread-like or transparent. Leeches are related to worms, but have suckers on each end and suck blood from fish or other small animals.

WORMS AND SNAILS

These creatures live amongst the water plants and also in the mud and decaying matter on the bottom of a pond.

Bristle worm

Whirlpool ram's horn snail

Flatworm

Leech

Many pond creatures are single-celled, and so small they can only be seen using a microscope. They mostly feed on tiny algae, but sometimes they eat one another.

THE LIFE OF A GNAT

The female gnat lays eggs in "rafts" on the water surface. Transparent larvae hatch and hang from the surface. They breathe through a tube within their tails. They sift the water for tiny pieces of food. The pupae also hang at the surface before changing to adults.

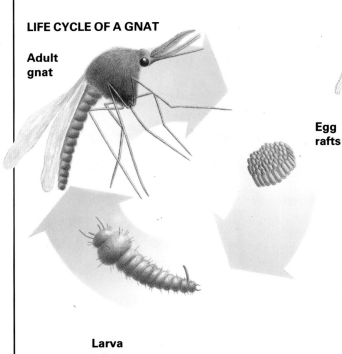

LIFE CYCLE OF A GNAT

Adult gnat

Egg rafts

Larva

INSECTS

Water scorpions and water stick insects live all their lives in water. The water boatman can fly from pond to pond. Dragonflies and mayflies live in water as nymphs but in air as adults.

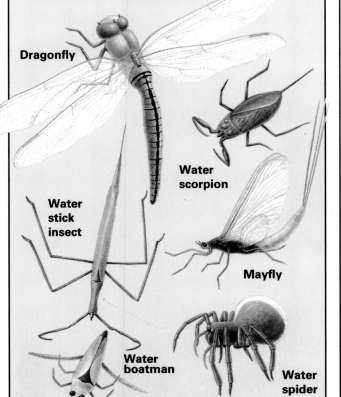

Dragonfly

Water scorpion

Water stick insect

Mayfly

Water boatman

Water spider

AMPHIBIANS

Most amphibians live on land as adults, but they return to water to lay their eggs. These eggs, called "spawn", hatch into larvae which swim and feed in water before they change, or "metamorphose", into adults.

In spring these adult amphibians go to ponds to breed. You may find their eggs. Frogs lay a jelly-like mass of spawn, whereas toads lay long strings of eggs. Newts and salamanders attach each egg separately to the leaf of a water plant. Amphibians often start life with feathery gills with which they can breathe under water, but these are lost as they become air-breathing adults.

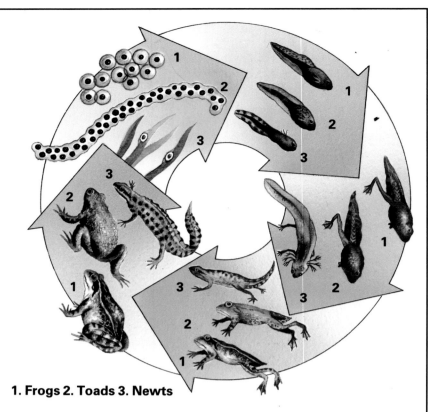

1. Frogs 2. Toads 3. Newts

FROGS, TOADS AND NEWTS

In warm climates amphibians abound in parks and gardens. Most are fairly secretive, until the mating season, when they are often extremely vocal, and hop or creep around in search of a mate.

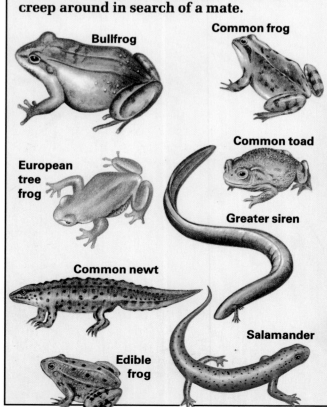

Bullfrog
Common frog
European tree frog
Common toad
Greater siren
Common newt
Salamander
Edible frog

COLLECTING FROG SPAWN

A few tadpoles can be kept in a jam jar, but an aquarium is better. Do not forget their food. Tadpoles eat algae at first, but start them off on bits of boiled lettuce and as they grow, offer them scraps of meat (tinned dog or cat food will do). Put in a little at a time so the remains do not foul the water. When tadpoles grow four legs they must be able to get out of the water. It is best to put them back in a pond at this time.

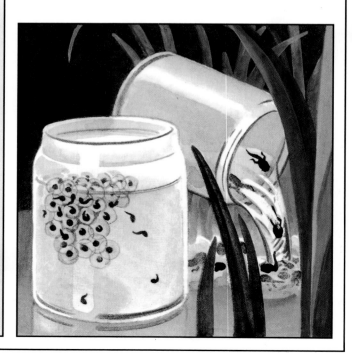

BIRDS

Water provides many kinds of food for birds. It is also a barrier that protects them from land enemies. A moorhen, when alarmed, can sink in the water like a submarine, leaving its beak up as a snorkel. Some birds visit the waterside to probe for worms and other small creatures in the surrounding mud. Others, like herons, stand patiently in the shallows, waiting for fish to come within striking distance. There are birds that stay on the surface, others that dive for food. If you are still and quiet you may notice where birds are nesting. Ducks and swans often nest close to the shore, whereas coots build nests that float on the water's surface.

IDENTIFYING POND BIRDS

Some waterbirds are easy to identify, such as swans or herons. Others, including sandpipers and other waders, may take practice to recognise. Look at overall shape, the length of beak, neck and legs, the shape of toes, where the bird is and what it is doing, as well as details of colouring.

Green sandpiper

Water rail

Kingfisher

Garganey duck

Canada goose

Baillons crake

Grey heron

Teal

Moorhen

Mute swan

FOOTPRINTS
Birds often leave tracks in the mud. You can identify them by checking if the feet were webbed, lobed, or had separate toes, as well as by size.

Cormorant

Swan

Coot

Pigeon

FEEDING BEHAVIOUR
Watch birds feeding. Each kind has its own way of hunting or eating, which is unique to the species.

MAKING A POND ENVIRONMENT

If you have a garden you can construct a real pond, but failing this a coldwater aquarium can be stocked with plants and animals to make a "natural" habitat. One secret of success is to make sure that the animals have enough oxygen. Choose an aquarium with a big surface, not one which is tall and narrow. Do not overcrowd it, and above all do not put in fierce hunters such as diving beetles and dragonfly larvae that will eat other insects and small fish.

FISH
Goldfish make good pond fish, as they can survive in stagnant water. Sticklebacks are found in all kinds of water. Minnows can live in ponds, but prefer clear moving water.

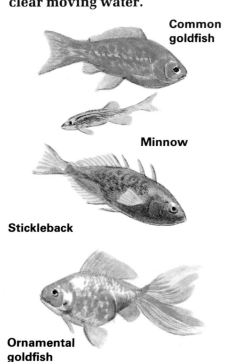

Common goldfish

Minnow

Stickleback

Ornamental goldfish

Canadian pond weed

Golden orfe

Arrowhead

PLANTS
Canadian pond weed is useful in pond environments because it puts oxygen into the water. Plants, such as those on the left, give growing and small animals somewhere to hide.

FROG SPAWN

You can follow a frog's growth from spawn (eggs) to tadpoles and then tiny frogs over about 12 weeks.

MOLLUSCS

Snails climb on the plants and over the sides of a pond. They eat the green algae that would otherwise grow rapidly cover these surfaces.

Frog spawn

Great diving beetle

Common snail

Stonefly nymph

Hornwort

INSECTS

Water insects include plant and meat eaters among the many kinds of beetles and bugs. They often arrive attached to new plants.

Great diving beetle

Water scorpion

Water-stick insect

WOODLAND LIFE

Woodland provides a shelter for its inhabitants. It shelters them from the extremes of weather. Wind speeds and temperature changes are usually less in a wood than outside. It can also allow animals to hide, sheltering them from enemies. The trees that are in a wood give it its main characteristics. Are they tall or low, evergreen or deciduous? How much do they shade the ground below? All these things affect how many shrubs and flowers grow in the wood, and also which animals will live there.

You can see plants and animals most easily at ground level, but do not forget that many birds, insects and other animals use parts of the tree high above the ground. Worms, insects, millipedes and many other animals live in the ground below, and in fallen trees.

WOODLAND MAP
You can make a ground-level map of part of the wood you choose to study. Show the tree trunks and the plants that cover the ground, as well as any features such as animal paths and burrows.

Sparrow hawks and stoats hunt across the glades and spaces in the wood. Small birds catch insects from the branches. Dead or dying trees are food for fungi and many insects. Birds such as woodpeckers feed on these. Woodmice and rabbits eat plants on the ground. They are hunted by weasels, foxes and owls that may swoop down.

Grey squirrel

Ground beetles

Great spotted woodpecker

Sparrow hawk

Badger

Bracket Fungi

Toadstools

Marsh worms

Fieldmouse

Rabbit

Weasel

Tawny owl

Norway spruce

Roe deer

Fox

WATCHING WILDLIFE

You stand little chance of seeing wildlife in a wood if you keep moving and making noises. But if you can stand or sit quietly in one place many animals will not notice you. A "hide" (see photo below) can be useful to conceal you, but mammals such as deer or badgers may still detect you as an intruder by your scent or the slightest noise.

Some animals sleep during the day. Deer become most active at dusk. Other woodland animals, such as badgers, move around at night, and are hidden in burrows during the day. Even if you cannot see animals, you may be able to detect their presence in a wood. Are there any pine cones chewed by squirrels or hammered by woodpeckers? Can you see any burrows? Are there paths running from these? There may be footprints in mud or snow. You may be able to recognise where a badger has scratched at a tree, or a deer has nibbled a plant the night before.

BROADLEAVES AND CONIFERS
Most conifers have needle-like leaves all the year. Broadleaved trees grow new leaves each spring and shed them in autumn (see below).

WINTER   SPRING   SUMMER   AUTUMN

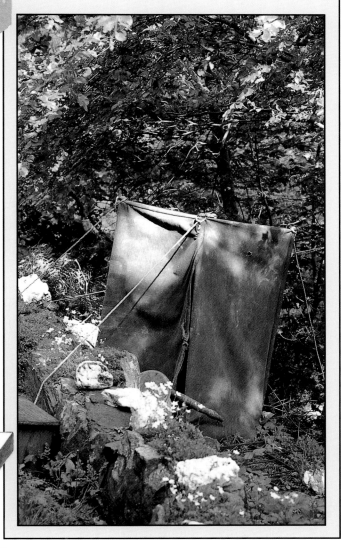

PLANTS AND TREES

The trees that grow in a wood affect all the other plants. Under a forest of conifers there will be little light and an acid soil. Only a few kinds of plant flourish there. Under the more open canopy of an oak wood many more kinds of plant can live. There may be shrubs such as hazel. Primroses, anemones and other flowers may carpet parts of the woodland floor. Smaller plants such as liverworts and mosses grow in damp places, and ferns too are part of the undergrowth. Fungi are not strictly plants, but these organisms are also an important part of the wood as they help dispose of rotting material. Many kinds of tree live in close association with a soil fungus and they seem to help one another. Keep a note of how often you find a certain toadstool under a particular kind of tree.

TREES

One way to tell trees apart is by their general shape. This is often easier to see in a park than a wood. Colours and textures of barks also differ greatly, but the easiest method of recognition is by leaf shape. Even conifers have different types of needles. The shapes and colours of flowers (such as catkins) and fruits (like acorns) are also useful.

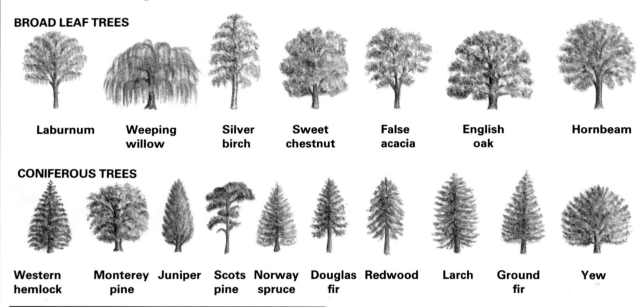

BROAD LEAF TREES

Laburnum   Weeping willow   Silver birch   Sweet chestnut   False acacia   English oak   Hornbeam

CONIFEROUS TREES

Western hemlock   Monterey pine   Juniper   Scots pine   Norway spruce   Douglas fir   Redwood   Larch   Ground fir   Yew

WILD FLOWERS

Many woods are filled with flowers in spring and summer. In some places they have become rare through picking.

Wood anemone

Blackthorn (bush)

Great butterfly orchid

Daffodil

Primrose

Strawberry   Bluebell

FUNGI

Invisible threads of fungi run through the soil. Toadstools and mushrooms, common in the autumn, are their spore-bearing parts.

Devil's boletus

Yellow staining mushrooms

Death cap

Fly agaric

Shaggy inkcaps

INSECTS

Insects abound in woodland. In summer the branches may be full of caterpillars feeding on the leaves. These are just one stage in the cycle of metamorphosis (changing of shape) in the lives of butterflies or moths. The diagram on the right illustrates the changes.

Many minute wasps live inside leaves and buds. They cause scars on the plant called galls. On oak leaves they create what are called "spangles" and other bumps, and on rose bushes they are responsible for "robin's pin cushions". The stag beetle, one of the largest beetles, relies on decaying wood for its food and a site for breeding.

LIFE CYCLE OF A BUTTERFLY

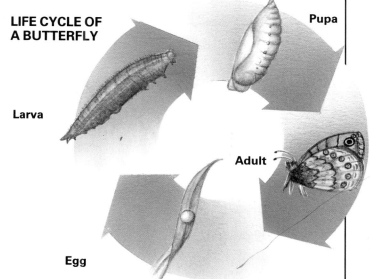

Pupa

Larva

Adult

Egg

BUTTERFLIES

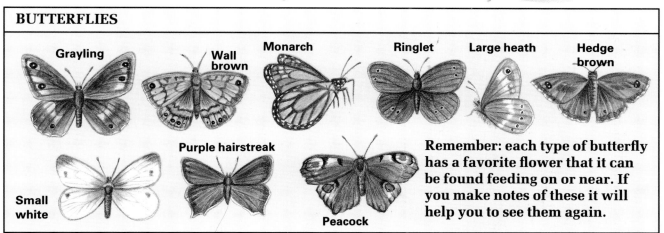

Grayling

Wall brown

Monarch

Ringlet

Large heath

Hedge brown

Small white

Purple hairstreak

Peacock

Remember: each type of butterfly has a favorite flower that it can be found feeding on or near. If you make notes of these it will help you to see them again.

SOIL CREATURES

Plant-eating millipedes and worms live in the woodland soil. Centipedes hunt their prey in the soil and leaf litter. Many beetles and other insects are at home here too.

Greater stag beatle

Sawfly

Longhorn beetle

Common wasp

Pot worms

Cockchafer beetle larva

Weevil

BIRDS

When you are watching or looking for birds, a pair of 8×30 binoculars is often helpful. Try to study singing birds and remember the sounds they make. This may help you recognise birdsong in the future. Listen for a woodpecker drumming on a tree, or the screech of a jay, as well as the songs of smaller birds.

More kinds of bird may be around in spring, when birds from colder climates come to breed. In winter birds may be easier to see, and some, like geese, move about in large feeding flocks.

DIFFERENT SPECIES OF BIRD

You can recognise birds by the way they behave. For example, woodpeckers climb treetrunks head up, while nuthatches scamper up or down the branches.

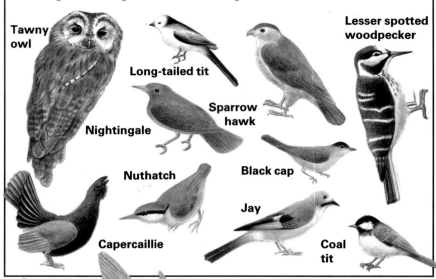

Tawny owl

Long-tailed tit

Nightingale

Sparrow hawk

Lesser spotted woodpecker

Nuthatch

Black cap

Jay

Capercaillie

Coal tit

DROPPINGS & PELLETS

Droppings on the ground may give a clue to a nest or roosting place above. Some bird's droppings, such as those of grouse, are easy to recognise. Some birds, including owls, herons and crows, bring up indigestible food remains through their mouths, in the form of a pellet. If you find these, little bones and bits of insects inside give a clue as to what the bird fed on.

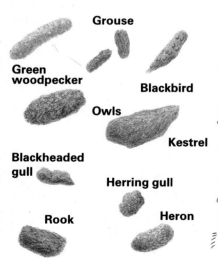

Grouse

Green woodpecker

Blackbird

Owls

Kestrel

Blackheaded gull

Herring gull

Rook

Heron

2.

1.

5.   4.   3.

1. Primary   2. Secondary   3. Down
4. Contour   5. Tail

BIRD FEATHERS
Feathers from various parts of a bird are different shapes and colours. You can tell where a fallen feather has come from (see examples below).

A jay's

A rook's

A hen pheasant's

BIRDS IN FLIGHT
Wing movements help you identify birds. Do they glide, hover, fly fast or slow, straight, or up and down?

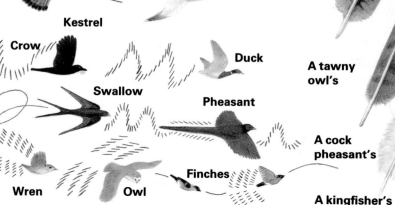

Gull

Kestrel

Crow

Duck

Swallow

Pheasant

A tawny owl's

Finches

Wren   Owl

A cock pheasant's

A kingfisher's

16

MAMMALS

Mammals are harder to study than birds. Many are shy and a large number spend the day asleep. Squirrels move about during the day, and you may see voles too. Shrews are active round the clock, rushing through their tunnels and the leaf litter. You may catch a glimpse of a weasel or stoat. Other mammals, like badgers, bats and foxes, are most likely to be seen in the late evening when they start their activity. It is often easier to detect a mammal's presence by signs it leaves behind. Nuts chewed in a particular way reveal woodmice. A carcase may show signs of a fox's feeding. The size of a burrow, or droppings nearby, can indicate its occupant. Fur and footprints are also revealing.

MAMMALS

Red fox

Grey squirrel

Red squirrel

Hedgehog

Mole

Raccoon

Bat

Edible dormouse

Deer

Vole

Badger

TRACKS

A good sharp footprint identifies its owner and shows which way, and how fast, an animal was moving. You can make casts of prints as shown in the stages below.

Put a cardboard ring around the print to start with.

Mix some plaster of Paris into water and pour in the mixture. Wait ten minutes for it to set.

Characteristic footprints of mammals are shown below.

Horse

Wild cat

Red deer

Dog

Sheep

Fallow deer

Rabbit

Edible dormouse

REPTILES

Reptiles are cold-blooded animals. This means that they do not make their own body heat, but gain it from the sun and their surroundings. Reptiles are common in warm places such as the American deserts. In cool climates they are active only in the summer and they hibernate underground in winter. Many reptiles are shy and avoid humans, but you may see them when they come out to bask in the sun.

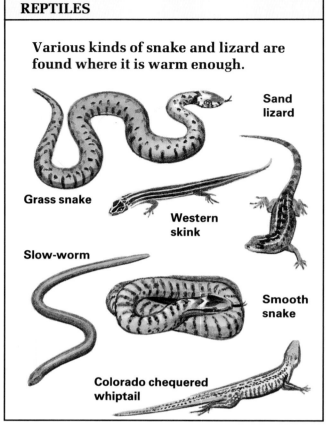

Grass snake

Sand lizard

Western skink

Slow-worm

Smooth snake

Colorado chequered whiptail

ADJUSTING TO THE HEAT
Reptiles spend much time adjusting their body temperature. They sunbathe morning and evening to get warm, but shelter from the excessive heat of the midday sun.

WARNING: NEVER LIFT ROCKS BY HAND

Adult

Eggs

Young lizard

REPTILE CHARACTERISTICS
Most reptiles live in dry holes or under logs. When they are not sunning themselves they may lurk in shade or amongst dense undergrowth. Since no snake likes being disturbed, and some are venomous, it is not advisable to turn over stones to look for them.

REPTILE HAUNTS

Shade

Undergrowth

Down holes

Under logs

18

MAKE AN ANTS' NEST

It can be fun to study insects in your own *formicarium*, or ants' nest (see diagrams). You need a solid tray and a sheet of glass to cover it. Roll some plasticine into moulds for tunnels and press them onto the glass (1). Fill the tray with wet plaster (2) and put the two together until the plaster sets. Remove the plasticine and replace the glass (3). Put pieces of meat and fruit in one of the tunnels (4) if you want to keep the ants inside, or leave an open pipe as a way that they can come and go. You can cover this with a plastic bottle (5) if you want to keep them in. Now go out and collect a colony of ants. They must all be the same species, a good guide to this is their colour. Make sure you get a large queen, as well as "workers".

Finally, always keep your *formicarium* covered with a cloth until you want to view it.

1.

2.

3.

4.

5.

Queen

Worker   Male
WOOD ANTS

Queen

Male   Worker
RED ANTS

Queen

Worker   Male
BLACK ANTS

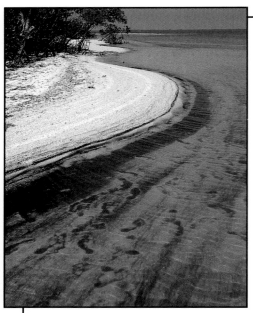

SEASHORE LIFE

The seashore is one of the harshest surroundings for living things. Twice a day these creatures are covered by water, then dry out as the tide goes out. They are exposed to heat, cold and buffeting waves. Conditions keep changing. But each tide brings in a new supply of food in the shape of microscopic sea creatures. In spite of the difficulties, many sea animals live on shores. Seaweeds grow among rocks where water is shallow enough to get the light they need. There is a huge number of kinds, but by observation and taking notes you will find you soon get to know the main ones. The seashore is one of the places that are most fun for a naturalist. There is always something to see, and you are never quite sure what will be in the next pool.

SHORE ZONES
If you map seaweed types on a rocky shore you will find they live at different levels on the beach. The same is true for many of the animals.

Laver

Limpets

Barnacles

Small periwinkles

Bladder wrack

Starfish

Lobster

Sea wrack

Shore crab

Whelks

SEARCHING THE BEACH

To discover which animals live along a shore, especially at the lower levels, follow the tide out down the beach. Many animals will have hidden in crevices and beneath rock ledges, others may be lurking in rocky tide pools, so you should be able to get close enough to study them.

Gulls are successful scavangers. You will see them swoop down to catch crabs or to gobble up any small fish that may have become tangled in seaweed and stranded by the tide.

Black headed gull

Sea bindweed

Hermit crab

Common dog whelks

VARYING TIDES
The height of the tides varies throughout a month, but parts of the shore are only wetted by the highest spring tides. Some sea creatures can survive where they are only just splashed by spray.

Splash zone

SPRING TIDE
HIGH TIDE
LOW TIDE

LARGER SPECIES

Seals swim near the shore and may climb out to rest if they don't see you. Dolphins and porpoises sometimes play close by the shore. Search the strandline for the remains of these and other dead animals washed up there after storms.

MAKING TRACKS
Seals are graceful swimmers but are clumsy on land. If they cross sand they may leave tracks like these.

Grey seal and tracks

Bottlenose dolphin

Pilot whale

Loggerhead turtle

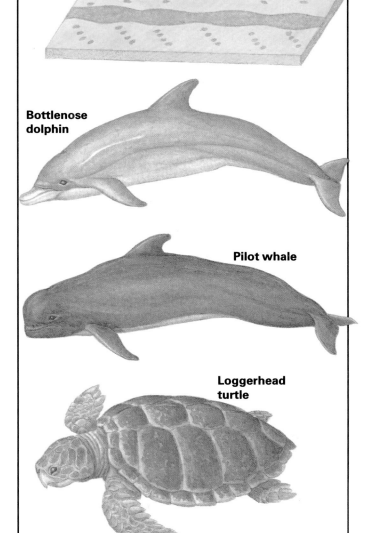

PLANTS

Sandy beaches above the high tide mark have their own plants, including the fleshy-leaved sea bindweed and the striking sea holly. Marram grass also grows on sand dunes, its roots binding the sand together.

Sea bindweed

Glasswort

Sea holly

Marram grass

Thrift

SEAWEEDS
The big oarweeds are only visible at the lowest tides. Laver is edible.

Bladderwrack

Oarweed

Irish moss

Laver

BIRDS

Terns fly above the water and swoop down for fish. Cormorants swim underwater to find prey. Waders such as curlew are most common on muddy shores where they probe for food. Gulls eat all kinds of food – watch for them flying up with crabs or shellfish and dropping them to crack their shells open on the rocks below.

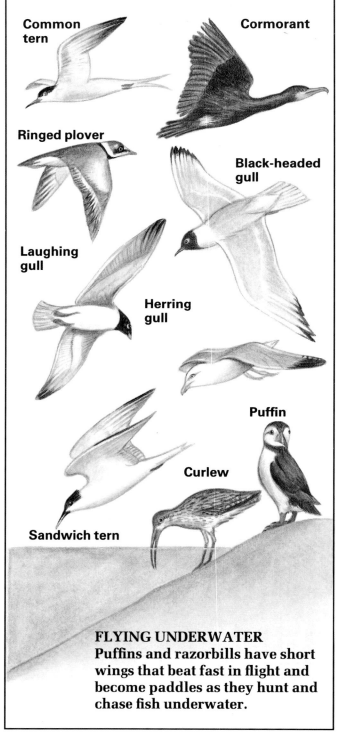

Common tern

Cormorant

Ringed plover

Black-headed gull

Laughing gull

Herring gull

Puffin

Curlew

Sandwich tern

FLYING UNDERWATER
Puffins and razorbills have short wings that beat fast in flight and become paddles as they hunt and chase fish underwater.

FISH

Sea fish are not often easy to see. In shallow water over a sandy bottom you may find flatfish like plaice or flounder. Other fish may be seen in clear water from piers and breakwaters, or may be fished out by anglers. You can sometimes find young fish, which have been killed by the violent waves of a storm, lying dead on the shore.

FISH

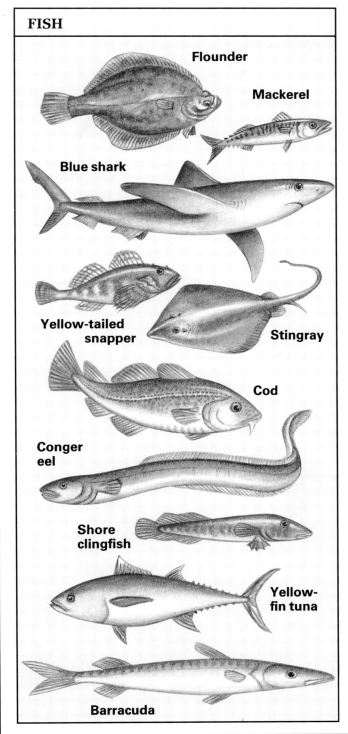

Flounder

Mackerel

Blue shark

Yellow-tailed snapper

Stingray

Cod

Conger eel

Shore clingfish

Yellow-fin tuna

Barracuda

LOOKING UNDERWATER
A glass-bottomed bucket, or a clear plastic box, helps you see into water without being disturbed by the reflections and roughness of the surface (see photo above).

Conger eel

Plaice

Grouper

SHORE FISH
Many fish are good at hiding under rocks and in crevices. Some fix themselves to rocks with suckers. Others can leap from one pool to another. Most are well camouflaged and hard to see unless they move.

SHELLED ANIMALS

Crustaceans have armoured and jointed skins to protect against the pounding seas and also against enemies. Their muscles lie inside and form the parts of a prawn, crab or lobster that we can eat. Most crustaceans are scavengers; they filter tiny pieces of food from the water to eat.

Echinoderms are animals such as starfish and sea urchins, that have tough spiny skins. Starfish are easy to recognise because most have five-rayed arms which radiate from their bodies.

The biggest group of shelled animals are the molluscs. They have soft bodies protected by hard shells. These may be single shells, as in winkles, or double (with a top and bottom) as in clams and mussels.

COMMON TYPES OF SHELLED ANIMALS

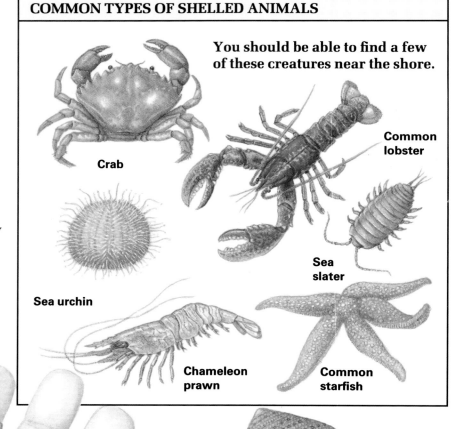

You should be able to find a few of these creatures near the shore.

Crab

Common lobster

Sea slater

Sea urchin

Chameleon prawn

Common starfish

Precious wentle trap

Florida worm shell

Strawberry top

Agar shell

Rough file clam

Tapestry turban

Pelican's foot

Blue-veined limpet

SEA SHELLS
Many empty shells are cast up on the shore especially after storms or very high tides. You can collect them without harming any living animals. Different kinds can be found all over the world.

ROCKPOOL STUDY

A rockpool is a miniature world of its own. Even in a small area there can be dozens of kinds of animal and many seaweeds. When you approach a pool try to keep your shadow from falling across it as that may frighten the animals. Remember that many creatures will be hidden among the weeds or under rocks and stones. Turn these over gently in your search. Always turn them back again as they were, so you cause as little long-term disturbance as possible. Animals and plants may survive only if they are on the right side of the rock.

Lobster

Limpets

Cockle

Barnacles

Rough winkle

Shrimp

Crab

Starfish

Lugworm

CATCHING CRABS
Except for deep pools, you will find short-handled nets easier to use than long ones. Handle all captured crabs carefully and return them to their pools.

POOL CENSUS
You can make a map of a small pool. Do not forget the barnacles and limpets on the rocks. Dig down into the sand.

IN TOWN

You can see plenty of wildlife in a town. Some animals have adapted well to human presence, or taken advantage of it. Martins and swallows choose the high and sheltered eaves of house roofs as places to nest – they are rather like the cliffs they would find in the wild. Bats roost in roof spaces or tiny crevices under the tiles. Pigeons and mice make use of the scraps left from human food. Large animals like foxes move into towns and scavenge amongst the rubbish at night. Even in cities there are large trees. Some of these, such as silver birch, are native species. Other trees, such as planes and monkey-puzzles have come from abroad but are planted because they are attractive and grow well in towns.

ANIMAL TRAFFIC SURVEY
Humans are not the only animals moving round the town. Track the routes taken by birds. Even on pavements you can plot ant trails.

Dove

Catkins

House mouse

Badger

Fox

Smoky bat

House martin

Mole

Daffodils

LIFE ON WALLS

On sunny walls small zebra spiders sun themselves and chase prey. Other spiders live in crevices . You can see their webs surrounding the entrances. Insects and mites are also attracted to a wall's warmth or to its dark hiding places. On damp walls moss and other small plants will grow. On neglected or broken walls there may be grass, flowers, or sapling trees that have taken root.

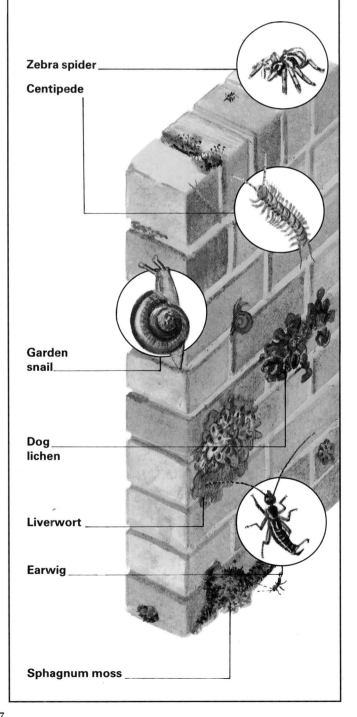

Zebra spider

Centipede

Garden snail

Dog lichen

Liverwort

Earwig

Sphagnum moss

GARDENS

With a mixture of trees, shrubs and low-growing plants, many gardens are rather like a woodland edge or glade. Animals that like that sort of surrounding, such as blackbirds, do well in gardens. Many birds will nest in hedges or bird boxes, even close to a house. Others may be attracted by bird tables. Insects and spiders will be almost everywhere that you care to look.

Small copper

Speckled wood

Swallowtail

BLACKBIRD'S NEST AND EGGS

Flowers

LADYBIRDS AND BEETLES

Ladybird

Common dor beetle

Devil's coach horse

All the insects and other animals that you can see here are attracted to the trees, flowers, nuts, roots and wildlife which are to be found in a garden.

MAMMALS

Fox

European mole

COMMON GARDEN SPIDERS

Garden spider

Harvestman

Crabspider

Woodmouse

BIRDS

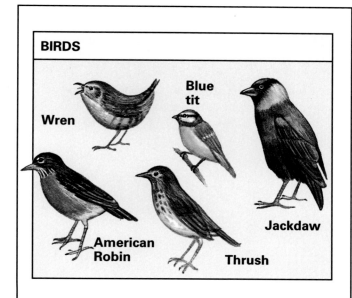

Wren

Blue tit

Jackdaw

American Robin

Thrush

A BIRD TABLE

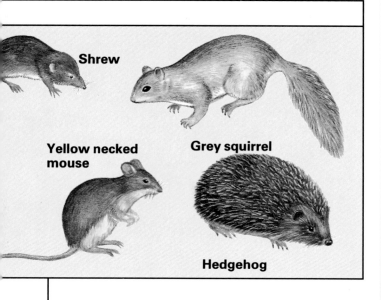

Shrew

Grey squirrel

Yellow necked mouse

Hedgehog

IN THE HOUSE

However clean and tidy a house is, there are dozens of small animals in it. Most are harmless and we never notice them. Some, such as clothes moths, are a nuisance. Others, cockroaches for example, spread germs if they get into food stores. Flies, fleas and lice cause other problems. Search window and door frames and corners to see what you can find in your home.

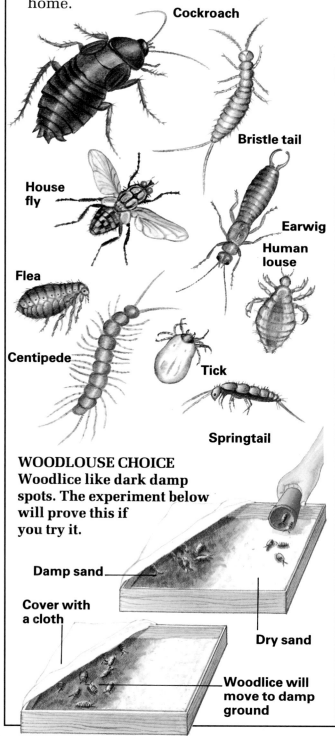

Cockroach

Bristle tail

House fly

Earwig

Human louse

Flea

Centipede

Tick

Springtail

WOODLOUSE CHOICE
Woodlice like dark damp spots. The experiment below will prove this if you try it.

Damp sand

Cover with a cloth

Dry sand

Woodlice will move to damp ground

KEEPING RECORDS

An important part of being a naturalist is keeping some sort of record of what you see. Your observations will be more interesting to you, and more valuable to others, if they are carefully recorded. The information could be anything from what month the plants flowered to what the weather and other conditions were when you saw a rare butterfly. Such information will be more reliable written down than in your memory, where details are gradually forgotten.

FILING RECORDS
A card index file with records in alphabetical order is a simple and good way of storing your naturalists notes and records.

DIFFERENT WAYS TO KEEP RECORDS
Some people keep a diary of their nature watching. If you want to be even more scientific you can record details of animals you have observed on index cards (see below).

LATIN NAME
NAME:
DATE SEEN:
HABITAT:
TIME OF DAY:
WEATHER:
WHAT WAS IT DOING:
SPECIAL NOTES:

Red
Black
Red

Habitat: Green Park
Time: 1.40 pm
Weather: Wind South west
Bright & clear
Wind Force F3 - 4

A FIELD NOTEBOOK
Carry a small notebook in your pocket. You can make a rough sketch of animals and plants you do not recognise, and make notes on colours. You can look them up later. You can also record details of places and conditions when you found things of interest.

EQUIPMENT

No piece of equipment is ever more important than your own senses, but other things do help. Binoculars are often useful but they should be light to carry, and a camera is a good way of recording details. A magnifying glass and plastic bags may help when examining and collecting small specimens.

Penknife

Binoculars

Storage containers

Torch

Field guides and books

Magnifying glass

Hat

Large pockets

Butterfly net

Strong boots

Water proof clothing

NATURALIST'S CODE

Everyone who is interested in nature will want to be careful about protecting it. Here is a list of do's and don't's.

Guard against all risk of fire.

Make no unnecessary noise.

Keep your dogs under close control.

Keep to public paths across farmland.

Use gates and stiles to cross fences, hedges and walls.

Take your litter home.

Help to keep all water clean.

GLOSSARY

algae simple water plants, including seaweeds and many single-celled kinds.
broadleaves trees with broad flat leaves, often deciduous.
conifers trees that produce seeds from cones. Most are needle-leaved.
environment the natural surroundings of an animal or plants in the wild.
food web the pattern of feeding that links living things together.
formicarium a container for captive ants.
habitat the place where an animal or plant lives.
larvae young forms of insects that hatch from eggs and grow to pupae.
metamorphose to change from one form to another.
nymphs young forms of some insects (mayflies, dragonflies) that gradually change to adult shape.
pupae insects in a resting stage between larva and adult forms.
segmented with a body made up of rings.
spawn name for the eggs of amphibians, fish and some other water animals.
species The classification of different types of animals. Only those of the same species can breed together.
spore-bearing producing single-celled spores to start a new plant, not seeds.
spring tides highest tides, occurring each month after new and full moons.
stagnant water that stands still, often low in oxygen.
stock to put into the water a supply of fish.
strandline the line reached by the highest tides, where rubbish from the sea is deposited.
webbed with skin stretched between the toes.
zones bands or areas with particular characteristics.

INDEX

Algae 7, 8
Amphibians 8
Ants 19, 26
Aquarium 8, 10

Badgers 13, 17, 26
Bats 17, 26
Beetles 14, 15, 28
Binoculars 16, 31
Bulrushes 5, 6
Burrows 12, 13, 17
Butterflies 15

Carp 5
Centipedes 15
Climates 8, 16
Conifers 13, 14
Cormorants 9, 22
Crabs 20, 22, 24, 25
Crustaceans 24

Deciduous 12
Deer 13, 17
Dolphins 21
Dragonflies 4, 7

Echinoderms 24
Eels 5
Eggs 7, 8, 11, 15, 18, 28
Environments 10
Equipment 11, 31
Evergreen 12

Feeding 8, 9, 12, 17, 19, 22
Fish 4, 10, 22, 23
Flowers 14, 27, 28
Formicarium 19
Foxes 17
Frogs 3, 4
Fungi 12, 14

Gills 8
Gnats 7
Goldfish 5, 10

Herons 9
Hibernation 4

Insects 4, 11, 12, 14, 27, 28

Larva 7, 15
Laver 20, 22
Leeches 7

Magnifying glass 11, 31
Mammals 17, 28
Mayflies 7
Metamorphosis 8, 15
Microscopic 7
Molluscs 11, 24
Moorhens 9,
Mushrooms 14

Newts 8

Oxygen 5, 10

Pellets 16
Ponds 4, 6, 7, 8, 9, 10, 11
Pools 3, 23, 25
Polaroid 4

Reeds 6

Reptiles 18
Roots 6

Salamanders 8
Seals 21
Seashore 20, 21
Seaweed 20
Shells 24, 25
Snails 11
Snakes 18
Spawn 8, 11
Species 9, 32
Spore 14
Sticklebacks 5, 10

Tadpoles 3, 8
Tides 20, 21, 22, 24
Toadstools 14
Trout 5

Water scorpions 7
Water stick insect 7
Worms 4, 7, 12, 15

Zones 6, 20

PRINTED IN BELGIUM BY
proost
INTERNATIONAL BOOK PRODUCTION